The 50 M
Roller Coaste

Nick Weisenberger

Copyright Information

First Edition – Paperback Version
Copyright ©2015 by Nick Weisenberger

ISBN-13: 978-1507785195
ISBN-10: 1507785194

Other Works by Nick Weisenberger

Coasters 101: An Engineer's Guide to Roller Coaster Design
The 50 Most Terrifying Roller Coasters Ever Built
Things to do in the Smokies with Kids
Once I was Adopted

Table of Contents

What Makes a Roller Coaster Unique?

Tired of the same old, rickety wooden roller coasters? Crave more thrills than the typical vertical loops and camelback hills found at every local amusement park? Fortunately, roller coasters come in all shapes and sizes. From innovative track designs to unusual seating configurations, from ridiculous locations to bizarre theming, riding these fear factories never gets old. *The 50 Most Unique Roller Coasters Ever Built* is a comprehensive list of unusual, rare, and hard to find scream machines.

So what's the definition of a "roller coaster"? Anything at an amusement park that makes you scream your head off, right? Not according to the coaster boys. A roller coaster is defined as a passenger carrying vehicle that rolls along one or more rails primarily due to gravity. The track does not necessarily have to be a complete, closed circuit. By this definition, "water slide coasters" (water slides that use rafts) are not included but "water coasters" that run on tubular steel rails are on this list. Other extreme amusement park rides such as freefall drop towers, water slides, swing rides, alpine coasters, etc. are not included.

There are over 3,000 roller coasters operating worldwide today, but what the average amusement park goer may not realize is many of them are "clones", rides that are the exact same. For example, RCBD lists fifty installations of Vekoma's boomerang coasters and forty-one suspended looping coaster (SLC) models. From the coaster manufacturer's perspective, this is a good business practice because it is cheaper to design one ride and sell it over and over again versus designing an entirely new ride every single time. A few standout coasters are 100 percent unique and as many are listed here as possible while at the same time still showing the full spectrum of ride types. So yes, a few coasters listed may not be 100% unique but their breed is still very rare and hard to find. For example, S&S Worldwide's 4th dimension coaster, while it is not 100% unique because there are currently three operating throughout the world, that's still pretty rare and chances are you will have to travel a long distance from your home base to ride one (plus they all have slight variations).

One category of ride has been completely left off this list - a relatively new breed of thrill ride is blurring the line between the traditional definition of a dark ride and a roller coaster. While these attractions truly are unique, the argument can be made they're not roller coasters, therefore I have omitted these from the list for now. A few examples of this new hybrid ride:

Arthur at Europa Park uses a vehicle that hangs below the rails of a coaster track and has gravity sections but is primarily electrically driven.

Harry Potter and the Escape from Gringotts is Universal Studios Orlando's latest groundbreaking attraction. It's another example of a vehicle that rides on coaster rails but is drive by drive tires. Some track sections also use motion base platforms that turn the coaster into a motion simulator attraction.

Wonder Mountain's Guardian at Canada's Wonderland features an outdoor coaster drop but is driven by tires most of the way through the indoor interactive scenes.

Blazing Fury at Dollywood and Fire in the Hole at Silver Dollar City have gravity driven drops but for the majority of the ride are driven by motors.

The 50 Most Unique Roller Coasters Ever Built is based upon the opinions of the author and not grounded in any scientific research. This book uses coaster and theme park terminology that I try to explain as I go but I've also included a glossary at the end of this book. I've tried to avoid as many duplicate coasters from my other book, *The 50 Most Terrifying Roller Coaster Ever Built*, but some could simply not be left off of this list (like Gravity Max). Coasters are ranked in reverse order, 50 to 1, with 1 being the most unique. Every ride includes pertinent information and stats such as name, location, height, inversions, etc. as well as an explanation for why it made this list.

***Spoiler Alert:** One of the most terrifying aspects of any thrill ride is the element of surprise. If you continue reading, the thrill of the attractions may be spoiled for you as each ride listed contains a description of the elements that make it terrifying and unique. Finally, onto the countdown...

The 50 Most Unique Roller Coasters Ever Built

50. FLASHBACK (Z-FORCE)

Known for: Only "Space Diver" coaster ever built
Park: Six Flags Magic Mountain, Six Flags Over Georgia, Six Flags Great America
Location: United States
Type: Steel
Opened: 1985
Closed: 2007
Designer/Manufacturer: Intamin
Height (ft): 86
Drop (ft): 34
Speed (mph): 35
Video: https://www.youtube.com/watch?v=JUdzb8Cl_68

1985 was the inception of a one-of-a-kind coaster, Z-Force. Specially crafted by Swiss engineers for Six Flags Great America, this ride was no walk in the park. Although there were no loops, there was a tempestuous vortex of precipitous drops and tight turns. The steep, twisting hairpin drops elicited the designers to dub this style of coaster a "space diver." The rolling over and diving maneuver was meant to recreate the feeling of flying a fighter jet. The four abreast seating of the five car trains was an uncommon feature in the 1980s (and wouldn't become popular until B&M started using four-across trains in the 1990s).

Z Force operated from 1988 to 1990 at Six Flags Over Georgia. After a year in storage, the coaster was relocated and renamed to Flashback at Six Flags Magic Mountain in 1992. However, Flashback barely operated while the adjacent water part was open due to the cacophony of sounds it produced when running. The condition of the track had also deteriorated with rust over the years causing passengers to complain about the rough ride. Flashback closed in 2003 and was left standing but not operating (SBNO). It was finally demolished in December of 2007 and sold as scrap.

Despite its compact size, the space diver model never caught on like the manufacturers were hoping. Today, you could say that S&S's El Loco coasters, with their small footprint and insane inversions, are the modern equivalent and evolution of this unique design (see Steel Hawg at Indiana Beach as an example).

49. HUNDEPRUTTERUTCHEBANE
Known for: Dog-flatulence-related theme
Park: BonBon-Land
Location: Denmark
Type: Steel
Opened: 1993
Designer/Manufacturer: Zierer
Height (ft): 14.8
Speed (mph): 18.6
Video: https://www.youtube.com/watch?v=oL8az1fV1Tw

Don't worry; I have a translation for the next ride on our list, Hundeprutterutchebane, although you may not believe me. Hailing from Denmark, this coaster is aptly named "Dog Fart Coaster". Trust me, it makes sense once you see it. Located in BonBon-Land, this is one of the many rides elegantly named to match wits with its candy creating owner, Michael Spangsberg. The name does fit as it is a children's ride, and who doesn't love to make children laugh? But

the creators took it a few steps further than just a silly name. The ride itself is a tame winding track with very minimal drops or speed. But there are two key components that make it a popular ride in the park. First, riders are sent through a small shed equipped with speakers that blast fart noises when a car passes through. I just hope they stopped with the noises, if you know what I mean. And if that isn't funny enough, the car then encircles a glorious statue of a dog lifting its leg and "pooping" with a few piles of perfectly sculpted feces on the ground below it. All in all, this ride will bring out the child in you. No stomach dropping, just jaw dropping. And no screams, just laughter.

48. FIORANO GT CHALLENGE
Known for: LSM racing coaster
Park: Ferrari World
Location: UAE
Type: Steel
Opened: 2010
Designer/Manufacturer: Maurer Söhne
Speed (mph): 59
Video: https://www.youtube.com/watch?v=VV1uU9cTUbo

The United Arab Emirates love auto racing and have been determined to bring the fast-paced track experience to visitors of all ages. They've succeeded with Fiorano GT Challenge at Ferrari World. This racing coaster features twin tracks, each with four separate LSM launch segments. The trains' three cars have been modeled after the styling of Ferrari F430 Spiders immersing passengers into the twisting, head-to-head varying speeds and accelerations of GT racing. The race wastes no time in getting started. A short drop out of the station leads into the first of the launch sections. An unusual feature is seeing how the curves have very little banking in order to simulate the lateral g forces felt by race car drivers. The desert region the park is located in has frequent sand storms; therefore goggles are issued to the guests to protect their eyes from the sand and bugs.

Fiorano GT Challenge uses a technology called LSMs to reach its top speed of nearly 60 miles per hour. Linear Synchronous Motors use the basic magnetism theories of attraction and repulsion. Strong, permanent, rare-earth (those which come out of the ground magnetized) magnets are attached to the train. Secured to the track are electro-magnets. When the train approaches one of the track-magnets, the track-magnet is set to attract the magnets on the train, pulling the train forward. After the train passes over the track-magnet, the track-magnet is reversed to repel the train magnet, pushing the train down the track. Multiple sets of electro-magnets on the track must be fired in sequence, switching polarity very quickly by the use of computers and electricity, in order to propel the train to top speed. Power for the ride system is provided via two flywheel motor generator sets, isolating the surge requirements of the launches from the electrical grid. But you won't be thinking about any of that when you're rocketed at scorching velocity through the desert. Race on!

47. COBRA

Known for: Designed by Pax
Park: Conny Land
Location: Switzerland
Type: Steel
Opened: 2010
Designer/Manufacturer: Pax Company
Height (ft): 137.8
Speed (mph): 52.8
Inversions: 2
Video: https://www.youtube.com/watch?v=P_bTt9m6NHg

Vekoma: 359, Intamin: 138, B&M: 103. These are the number of roller coasters designed by the most popular and well known roller coaster design firms. Cobra, the next coaster on our list, comes from a relative unknown company in the coaster world. Pax Company has created just three rides over 100 feet tall. According to the Pax Company website, it has discontinued all of its roller coaster models as of 2013 and now only manufactures Ferris wheels, so the few coasters they have produced will become even rarer.

Pax Company's crowning achievement is Cobra, a steel shuttle coaster where the track is not a complete circuit. After boarding and pulling down the over-the-shoulder-restraints, our train is dragged slowly backwards out of the station. We're pulled vertically so that we're staring straight down at the ground below. Without warning, the train is released; we plummet down the vertical spike, and rocket through the loading platform. After hurtling over two tummy tickling camelback hills we shoot into a tight vertical loop. Screams rise from our throats instinctively as we hit the "scorpion tail" inversion – a nearly-half vertical loop where the track suddenly straightens out and keeps going. We climb in height all the while still upside down! When we lose momentum, and are clinging to our harnesses, we fall backwards and repeat the process, but at a slightly slower speed so that we're just crawling over the now airtime-less hills. As soon as we begin to doubt we may not make it the train glides back into the loading platform and our harnesses release. You may need a breather before you decided to do that one again.

46. REAPER, DROP RIDE TO DOOM
Known for: e-Motion coaster in a unique location
Park: Amsterdam Dungeon
Location: Netherlands
Type: Steel
Opened: 2005
Closed: 2014
Designer/Manufacturer: Mack Rides
Height (ft): 22.7
Speed (mph): 15.7
Video: https://www.youtube.com/watch?v=ylel4K1NYAc

Reaper: Drop Ride to Doom had one of the most unique ride locations ever - inside a real 13th century church! Themed to the Grim Reaper legend, Drop Ride to Doom provided a climatic finale to the Amsterdam Dungeon experience. Not only that, but it was only one of two Mack Rides e-Motion roller coasters ever built. The selling point of the e-motion coaster is a ride vehicle that is constructed to enforce the feeling of being thrown out of the car while whipping around hairpin turns. This unique sensation is created because the six person vehicles have a spring suspension allowing it to rock and tilt to the sides. And the noteworthiness doesn't end there. Among Reaper's many idiosyncrasies is a vertical elevator lift similar to the one used on Lost Coaster at Indiana Beach. And that's not all! *Reaper* also features a reversing track segment comparable to the ones found on Universal's Revenge of the Mummy coasters. Space was tight inside the former chapel so the steel was twisted into an ultra-compact layout. Unfortunately for roller coaster junkies, this unique experience closed permanently on January 5th, 2014.

45. VERBOLTEN

Known for: Freefall drop section
Park: Busch Gardens Williamsburg
Location: United States
Type: Steel
Opened: 2012
Designer/Manufacturer: Zierer
Drop (ft): 88
Speed (mph): 53
Video: https://www.youtube.com/watch?v=k0zN_Hjbmqc

Verbolten – a play on the word verboten, meaning "forbidden" - is a Zierer manufactured multi-launching steel roller coaster at Busch Gardens Williamsburg. We board one of five trains that hold sixteen passengers, each adorned with bright colors and working headlights. The journey to the Black Forest begins with a few leisurely turns before we hit the first launch pad. As we pick up speed, we're catapulted inside a dark show building and greeted by a foreboding forest. The inside of the event building is decorated with painted drops and set pieces, as well as featuring unique sound and lighting effects to give us the feeling we've entered an area we're not supposed to be in.

After dancing around in the dark, our car slows down and halts on a flat, straight piece of track. Here we'll experience one of three randomized story lines:

1. A lightning storm with fierce flashes of light threatens to destroy us
2. An evil forest spirit will attempt to prevent us from ever leaving the forest
3. An attack by a pack of red-eyed wolves

You'll have to ride Verbolten at least three times to see all three of the alternating special effects driven story lines. What happens next is the main reason Verbolten makes it on this list: the free-fall track element. The section of track our train is stopped on suddenly detaches and plummets, straight down like a drop tower ride, temporarily lifting our stomach into our throats. This surprising element is pure laugh out loud fun.

Once our fall is halted, there's no time to catch our breaths. The track reconnects and we're shot out of the show building at 53 miles per hour via electro magnets. A quick elevated turn leads us to a rickety old bridge perched on top of a ravine. Far below is the blue of the majestic Rhine River. This is the exact same spot of the famous river plunge drop on the Big Bad Wolf suspended coaster that was removed to make way for Verbolten, a nice tribute to the former fan favorite. We perch at the top of the 88 foot ledge before diving down to the river. A large s-turn leads us back up the ravine and into the station. It's classified in coaster parlance as a "family ride" but you can be the judge of that.

44. HADES 360

Known for: Longest underground tunnel
Park: Mt. Olympus Water & Theme Park
Location: United States
Type: Wood
Opened: 2005
Designer/Manufacturer: The Gravity Group
Height (ft): 136
Drop (ft): 140
Speed (mph): 60
Inversions: 1
Video: http://youtu.be/xFhj4mVWCSY

According to the Roller Coaster Database, there are approximately 3,000 roller coasters operating worldwide today. Of these, only 172 (or 6.14%) are classified as "wood" coasters. The difference is primarily based on the material the rails are constructed from and not what the supports are made of. Generally, steel roller coasters are defined as a roller coaster with track consisting of tubular steel rails while wooden coaster tracks are made from layers of laminated wood. Hades at Mount Olympus, despite having a mostly steel support structure, is the first wooden coaster on our list. The rails are composed of eight pieces of wood stacked on top of each other and that's what makes it fall into the wood category.

Originally opened as simply "Hades" in 2005, this diabolical coaster was transformed in 2013 into Hades 360 with the addition of a 360-degree roll and a 110 degree overbanked turn. In order to help negotiate the newfangled maneuvers the coaster also received new state-of-the-art Timberliner trains from GravityKraft, sister company of the Gravity Group, the original designers of the ride. Hades 360 remains the only traditional track wooden roller coaster to go upside-down.

Unsuspecting riders are surprised to find out the most outlandish feature of the ride isn't the inversion - it's the 800 feet of underground tunnel, the world's longest on a coaster. The trains plummet down the 140 foot drop into complete darkness as they travel under Mount Olympus' parking lot, experiencing many dips and twists and a ninety-degree banked turn before emerging back into daylight only to find themselves upside-down. Without pausing even for a second, the action continues as the trains plunge back underground to travel under the parking lot again. The trains emerge into daylight again into a tall camel back next to the lift hill that will have you wondering if the ride breaks the laws of physics. How the trains have enough momentum to make it over a few more airtime hills and helix after all that is a mystery, but one thing we know for sure is it's certainly a terrifying and unique ride experience.

43. COP CAR CHASE
Known for: Indoor/outdoor racing coaster
Park: Movie Park Germany
Location: Germany
Type: Steel
Opened: 1996
Closed: 2006
Designer/Manufacturer: Intamin
Inversions: 2
Video: https://www.youtube.com/watch?v=KtD1hwaTisk

A heated pursuit between two racing coaster cars, but with real fire. How does that sound? Now add a couple inversions and you have yourself a really wicked ride. Up until it's closing in 2006, Cop Car Chase (original Lethal Weapon Pursuit) could be found in Germany's Movie Park. And it really was a pursuit, coaster style. Two separate tracks following similar ride paths had double the riders, and double the fun. Since each track is different, it's a two-for-one deal. You couldn't just choose one track without then trying the other. When one sends you up high, the other drops to ground level, but both send you into an abandoned looking building with labels "elevator one" and "elevator two" for either car to enter. The building's lack of lighting meant riders could barely see the oncoming loop until it was too late. And an intense loop it was, being more circular than the g-force reducing tear drop shape primarily used on modern coasters.

Upon exiting the building, there is a blast of fire in the shape of a horse running overhead. Riders actually said they could feel the heat of it, too. But it wouldn't be a real movie pursuit if the cops didn't lose their target, and this ride is no exception. The ride breaks apart into separate directions and sends either car into a whipping barrel row before coming together again to a slowed halt at the end. If a Hollywood speed chase came to life, it would definitely be this ride. Explosions and all.

42. VEIL OF DARK

Known for: Shooting dark ride/coaster combination
Park: Joypolis
Location: Japan
Type: Steel
Opened: 2012
Designer/Manufacturer: Gerstlauer
Height (ft): 16.4
Speed (mph): 23.6
Inversions: 1
Video: https://www.youtube.com/watch?v=KqOnvDdIFWs

What do you get when you mix Japan with thrill rides? A brand-spankin' new idea for roller coasters that mixes inversions with involuntary spins, that's what. Located in Tokyo's Joypolis, Veil of Dark is like a teacup ride from hell, in the best way possible. It starts off as a simple dark ride shooter where riders use remotes built into their shoulder restraints to aim at projection screens on either side of the track. Then the game comes to life. After shooting at the screen, the riders are shot into the ride of their lives as the four-person car is launched into a sudden inversion. If that isn't enough, the car also spins on its own, so not only are they upside down, but they're spinning around too. And it won't stop until the ride comes to an end.

Veil of Dark is the first coaster to combine the spinning motion of the vehicle with a barrel roll inversion in the track – easily one of the most disorienting elements ever devised. Japan is known for their crazy thrill rides and this is just the first of many on the unique coasters list.

41. BATTLESTAR GALACTICA
Known for: The only sitdown vs. inverted dueler
Park: Universal Studios Singapore
Location: Singapore
Type: Steel
Opened: 2010
Closed: 2013 (expected to reopen in 2015)
Designer/Manufacturer: Vekoma
Height (ft): 140
Speed (mph): 56
Inversions: 5
Video: https://www.youtube.com/watch?v=jWJYeimZUPo

Battlestar Galactica: Human vs. Cylon is a pair of steel, dueling roller coasters at Universal Studios Singapore. One of the coasters is an inverted roller coaster in blue, and the other half is a traditional seated roller coaster in red. There are seven near miss moments where the dueling trains come within feet of each other. The inverted side is a bit more intense and features all five inversions while the sit-down side is gentler and more of a "family" coaster with no inversions. It's amazing how much track is crammed into so small of a space.

Recently, the world's tallest dueling coaster is undergoing an extensive overhaul. Battlestar Galactica: Human vs. Cylon has had its fair share of problems since opening in 2010 and has actually been closed since July of 2013. Universal has only officially stated the ride is closed "for an attraction review" but it seems like they are going to give the ride a fresh start with a new identity and theme. The revamped ride is expected to get a new name, new interiors and a fresh coat of paint, among other proposed changes. This unique creation is the only dueling coaster in the world where one side is inverted and the other is a standard sit down vehicle, so it's good news to hear the ride is being revamped and not completely torn down. The update will take a couple of months and the coasters are expected to reopen in 2015.

40. JET RESCUE
Known for: steel launched jet ski roller coaster
Park: Sea World
Location: Australia
Type: Steel
Opened: 2008
Designer/Manufacturer: Intamin
Height (ft): 20
Speed (mph): 43
Video: https://www.youtube.com/watch?v=if4d6Vti5E0

When people hear "Sea World", they probably think of Shamu. But this ride hails from Down Under, in Sea World Australia (not associated with the SeaWorld parks in America). Fittingly named Jet Rescue, this fast paced ride imitates the jet ski rescue of a sea lion done by Sea World's Research and Rescue Foundation. Riders are strapped into jet ski shaped cars in pairs and are launched into constant twists and turns, reaching speeds of 70km (43mph). The key feature of Jet Rescue is its use of two launches instead of the standard one. The second launch occurs when the car enters a tunnel filled with a thick cover of mist, making it impossible for riders to see the track ahead. Once they pass over the launch pads, the car is shot out of the tunnel and into an unexpected turn followed by four more direction changes as they encircle an animatronic sea lion in need of "rescuing". The duration is around 30 seconds, but the speed it reaches paired with the elevated seating of the cars is enough to make your heart skip a beat.

39. SCOOBY-DOO SPOOKY COASTER

Known for: Surprise elements
Park: Warner Bros. Movie World
Location: Australia
Type: Steel
Opened: 2002
Designer/Manufacturer: Mack Rides
Height (ft): 56
Drop (ft): 23
Speed (mph): 27.7
Video: https://www.youtube.com/watch?v=nwLtwrUL7Pl

Fully enclosed roller coasters are no longer the rarest of novelties. One of the most innovative is Scooby-Doo Spooky Coaster, themed to the 2002 live action film Scooby Doo movie which was filmed at the studio adjacent to the park while constriction was ongoing. For the ride's hardware, Warner Bros. Movie World turned to manufacturer Mack Rides and ordered a custom wild mouse style coaster with more twists than an Agatha Christie novel.

Passengers board single vehicles that seat four victims at a time. With lap bars firmly in place, the adventure begins with a series of hairpin turns and small bunny hops through darkly-lit castle corridors and some animated, spooky effects pop out at the riders. After careening around the dark the car reaches the elevator lift. Two cars are loaded into the elevator to be lifted skyward at the same time – how's that for efficiency? As the cars climb to the fifty foot level, the unsuspecting passengers are tilted at an angle from one side to the other, like a rocking boat on stormy seas. When they reach the apex, the car is ejected backwards out of the elevator down a sudden drop. Back on a flat track, the car is rotated on a turntable to face forwards again before being pushed out and into the dark.

The car rips around the first horizontal 180-degree turn, the lateral forces slamming everyone on board to the right. Too bad it's so dark you can't see your hand before your face, because there's no way to brace for - *Whoa!* Another mad reversal of direction, this time to the left. Skittering through the gloom, the cars zoom back around, turning on a dime. At this point it's a standard wild mouse layout indoors in the dark with tight turns and small drops but that doesn't mean it's not super fun.

38. FURIUS BACO
Known for: World's only launched wingrider
Park: Port Adventura
Location: Spain
Type: Steel
Opened: 2007
Designer/Manufacturer: Intamin
Height (ft): 46
Speed (mph): 83.9
Inversions: 1
Video: https://www.youtube.com/watch?v=JO7BMbC_gSg

Furius Baco was the world's first wing coaster where the seats are cantilevered off the side of the train instead of being on top of or below the rails. This arrangement allows passenger's feet to dangle freely. Furius Baco may be the only roller coaster in the world themed to wine making. The middle of the train looks like wooden wine barrels and "Baco" is the Spanish word for Bacchus, the god of the grape harvest. The designers may have drunk a little too much wine while conjuring up this beast.

Additionally, what makes Furius Baco even more unique is it's the world's only launched wing coaster. While almost every other launched coaster typically launches immediately into a giant hill, Furius Baco races off of the launch track and dips down into a trench. The extreme 83 mile per hour speed is created by using a hydraulic launch. This system utilizes a catch car, called a sled, connected to a cable which latches on to a mechanism attached to the underside of the coaster train. The catch-car moves in its own track or "groove" in the center of the launch track. The hydraulic motor is located at one end of the launch track and the waiting train at the other. Think of it like a giant fishing pole that reels a train in super-fast before being released.

Furius Baco's profile stays low to the ground so the speed is maintained throughout. The sides of the trenches enhance the sense of speed, thus making the experience that much more intense. But because the wingspan of the vehicles is so wide the outside seats are far away from the center of gravity of the trains and often result in a rough and bumpy ride. This could be one of the reasons why Furius Baco has been the only wing-rider with stationary seats sold and manufactured by Intamin. The wing-rider market is dominated now by B&M who appears to have solved the roughness problem (and is launching their first launched wing coaster in 2015).

37. FIRECHASER EXPRESS

Known for: Unique station arrangement
Park: Dollywood
Location: United States
Type: Steel
Opened: 2014
Designer/Manufacturer: Gerstlauer
Speed (mph): 34.5
Video: https://www.youtube.com/watch?v=h7MZ0ti2Gk8

FireChaser Express at Dollywood is an innovative, new family coaster with a unique station arrangement. The Gerstlauer built coaster occupies the site of the former Adventure Mountain climbing attraction and even reuses some of the thematic elements. Not only does the ride feature two launches, it also has a chain lift hill up the side of the mountain. The coaster is themed around a volunteer fire station and the queue line and surrounding areas feature many little details to support the storyline. Unlike most roller coasters, the three, seven-car trains enter and exit the station from the same side. Just like a real fire truck might do, the vehicles back into the station and launch straight out of it.

FireChaser Express is pure laugh-out-loud fun. The layout takes the best elements from several other types of roller coasters and combines them into one great ride. There are wild mouse-style hair pin turns that press you into the side of your seat, tummy tickling airtime hills, trick-track, and a show scene complete with fire and smoke effects. It's a much more thrilling ride than other themed family coasters, namely Disney's Big Thunder Mountain, Universal's Flight of the Hippogriff, and Cedar Fair's Backlot Stunt Coasters. It's a great introduction to g-forces, something most family coasters lack.

Even for riders who aren't fans of traveling backwards on roller coasters, FireChaser Express hits the sweet spot of just enough thrills without being too long or uncomfortable. In fact, some would argue it's far more fun and effective than the backwards segments on other famous family coasters such as

Animal Kingdom's Expedition Everest and Universal Orlando's Revenge of the Mummy: The Ride. For the best thrills, sit in the back seat because you can see the other rider's reactions during the backwards segment. The sensations also change as you suddenly become the "front" of the train. FireChaser Express proves a coaster doesn't have to be the biggest or fastest to provide the most fun.

36. BANDIT BOMBER

Known for: On-board water drop
Park: Yas Waterworld
Location: UAE
Type: Steel
Opened: 2013
Designer/Manufacturer: Vekoma
Height (ft): 75.5
Speed (mph): 31.1
Video: https://www.youtube.com/watch?v=4Q2NMOOfiB8

Yas Waterworld is a new water park and may be the most impressive one ever built. Gargantuan water slides tower over other slides while monolithic rockwork protrudes through the gaps between the slides. Winding in and out of this spaghetti bowl of slides and supports is the Bandit Bomber, a "splash party" coaster designed by Vekoma. The four-passengers per suspended vehicle use on-board laser guns to trigger effects on the ground, such as geysers and water jets. But patrons on terra firma can fight back using their own water cannons, jets, geysers, and waterfalls. You're not going to get wet on this ride; you're going to get soaked!

The thrills of the splash party come from the interactivity. The coaster has two lift hills that each lead to a series of leisurely spirals and dips. Previous attempt at making an interactive water coaster, like Setpoint's Roller Soaker at HersheyPark, haven't had long term success due to issues like low capacity. Bandit Bomber appears to have remedied all those concerns and looks primed to be replicated at water parks the world over.

35. MOMONGA
Known for: 2-in-1 stand-up and sitdown trains
Park: Yomiuriland
Location: Japan
Type: Steel
Opened: 1979
Designer/Manufacturer: Togo
Height (ft): 82
Inversions: 1
Video: https://www.youtube.com/watch?v=v17M996pjwc

It's time to return to the land of the rising sun for another crazy roller coaster. Momonga at Yomiuriland may not look too unusual just looking at the track, but once you see it in action you'll realize they're using both a standup train and a sit-down train on the same track. Coaster enthusiasts have long debated whether or not a standup roller coaster could be converted to a sitdown coaster. The answer might have been sitting in Japan all along. Momonga began operation as just a sit-down roller coaster and never would have made this list. But after a similar ride at a competing park opened in 1982, a standup train was quickly added giving riders the option to ride sitting down or standing up. This quirky feature is about the only thing that keeps the short ride interesting. The lift hill threads through the middle of the lone vertical loop and the ride climaxes in a tight helix. You have to do it twice to get the full experience of sitting and standing and can decide for yourself which one is better. Momongo may have indirectly set the precedent for transforming Mantis at Cedar Point, from standup to a sitdown floorless coaster known as Rougarou.

34. BATMAN AND ROBIN: THE CHILLER

Known for: Dueling LIM Shuttle Loop Coaster
Park: Six Flags Great Adventure
Location: United States
Type: Steel
Opened: 1998
Closed: 2007
Designer/Manufacturer: Premier Rides
Height (ft): 200
Drop (ft): 140
Speed (mph): 65
Inversions: 4/2
Video: https://www.youtube.com/watch?v=2VUGZzPBD0s

One of the first really innovative racing/dueling coasters was Batman and Robin: The Chiller. The dynamic duo made a perfect fit to theme the high speed coasters and was timed to coincide with the release of the Batman & Robin movie. The film was a flop at the box office bringing the Batman movie franchise to a grinding halt (until Christopher Nolan revived it). Ironically, Batman and Robin: The Chiller didn't fare much better, being plagued with problems from the very start. The coasters were expected to open in summer of 1997. After multiple issues and delays, the opening was finally pushed back to the 1998 season.

The Chiller was just the third LIM launch coaster produced by Premier Rides. Linear Induction Motors use multiple sets of high powered electromagnets secured to the track. A gap is left in-between each set. Alternating current (AC) is applied to the magnets to create a magnetic field. A metal fin attached to the bottom of the train passes through the gap in the magnets while the magnetic field creates a wave for the fin to ride and propels or slows the train. In 1996, the Flight of Fear at Kings Island became the first roller coaster to use LIMs.

While the ride was SBNO for much of its life, at least it was interesting to look at. The Batman side's track was painted a dark blue and featured a139 foot towering inverted top hat element. The

Robin contrasted it nicely with a bright red track that wrapped around the top hat in a 105 foot tall double inverting t cobra roll. Next, the two tracks twisted side by side through an elevated barrel roll before reaching towards the heavens. It was unusual seeing coaster track just end in the middle of the sky.

Once the Chiller finally opened in 1998 the problems persisted. Frequent downtime was caused by waiting for parts to be repaired or modified. The ride was originally designed to duel, with both trains launching simultaneously, but power problems meant that was impractical, and the trains were launched in a staggered fashion for the few times in its history that both sides were running.

Another problem involved the trains valleying or saddling. This occurs when a coaster doesn't have enough momentum to make it up a hill or through an inversion, and gets stuck in a low spot. The train would usually valley between the spike and the tower, but occasionally could stop in the in-line twists or in the valley of Robin's cobra roll. Evacuation platforms would later be added to those low spots to aid getting the passengers off safely in the event of a train saddling.

At the end of the 2006 season, the future of The Chiller looked bleak, and rumors swirled that its days were numbered and it would be removed in the off-season. It looked like the ride was going to be removed when fans spotted a few sections of track had been taken off. The removal was part of a re-profiling effort in which the ride's barrel rolls were removed and replaced with new track. In spring of 2007, reconstruction of the Chiller tracks was underway, with the modified support structure in place and the Robin track in place. The Robin side did reopen in 2007 sans the barrel roll element, the inversion replaced by simple hump meant to reduce strain on the riders and vehicles

But this change didn't solve all the operational problem, low capacity, constant maintenance and the ride was promptly closed again. Deconstruction on the troubled ride began in September 2007. All the tracks and supports were removed. Will The Chiller be resurrected? The track pieces currently sit in storage at Beto Carrero World in Brazil.

33. HIGH ROLLER
Known for: Built on top of a tower
Park: Stratosphere Tower
Location: United States
Type: Steel
Opened: 1996
Closed: 2005
Designer/Manufacturer: Premier Rides
Drop (ft): 20
Speed (mph): 30
Video: http://www.youtube.com/watch?v=OgswFsHIkeg

High Roller could be considered the forefather of Vegas thrill rides. It was a spectacular concept, but the execution didn't exactly have the "wow" factor the creators expected. Compared to the other scream machines on this list, the High Roller wasn't much more than a kiddie coaster with its small drop, relatively slow speed, and uninspiring layout. What made it terrifying was its placement on top of the 1149-foot tall Stratosphere tower. The High Roller's bright red track wrapped around the tower at the 909-foot mark, level 12A, making it the highest in the world.

However, since it was connected to the tower, it couldn't go too fast without risking the integrity of the building. On top of that, the drop from top to bottom was a whopping 20 feet. The ride itself consisted of loops around the Stratosphere tower, slowly descending, and then ascending again for a second revolution. Riding in the outer seat, the one closest to the edge of the building, was a truly frightening experience. Yet many dare devils claimed the ride was boring or too bumpy. Shut downs due to high wind were very frequent. In the end, High Roller closed in 2005 to make way for newer, cutting-edge attractions on top of the tower that may be even more terrifying than High Roller was.

32. SCREAMING SQUIRREL
Known for: Saxophone elements and horizontal turns
Park: Wonder Island
Location: Russia
Type: Steel
Opened: 2007
Designer/Manufacturer: S&S Worldwide
Height (ft): 150.9
Inversions: 2
Video: https://www.youtube.com/watch?v=mp8-4ACJDJg

This next coaster sends us to Wonder Island in Russia. And it's no wonder it made the list. Screaming Squirrel is a "screaming squirrel" model coaster, meaning it goes upside down for prolonged periods by twisting under itself, known as a saxophone inversion. The ride begins with a steep, diagonal lift to the 151 ft. peak, then sends the four-person car over the edge into a perfect 90 degree drop. If staring directly at the ground doesn't send your stomach to your throat, then the ride shifts into a 100 degree curve. That's right. 90 degrees, nearly parallel to the ground, back to 90 degrees, then it slowly levels out. You're given two quick right turns to brace yourself for round two of floating off of your seat. Not only that, but it takes its sweet time doing it. They *really* want you to savor the gravity defying moments, so the ride actually *slows down* as it goes over the curve. If you're looking for a jaw, and stomach, dropping experience, look no further than Screaming Squirrel.

Wonder Island's ride is unique in that it appears to be somewhat of a transition ride between S&S Worldwide's older screaming squirrel models and their newer El Loco style rides like Steel Hawg at Indiana Beach. The original screaming squirrel models lack bank curves in their layouts, while the new El Loco model is much more versatile, with more comfortable seats as well. Therefore, this one very well could be the last screaming squirrel model ever built.

31. JET STAR II
Known for: Spiral lift and inline seating
Park: Lagoon Park
Location: United States
Type: Steel
Opened: 1976
Designer/Manufacturer: Schwarzkopf
Height (ft): 44.3
Drop (ft): 42
Speed (mph): 45
Video: https://www.youtube.com/watch?v=C9VQckRVDVE

Jet Star 2 was originally built at Riverfront Park in Spokane, Washington for Expo '74. It operated from May to November of that year before being relocated to Lagoon where it has been thrilling riders since 1976. Originally manufactured by the Anton Schwarzkopf Company, the track was partially rebuilt by Fabri-Weld in 1991. The ride is unique in the fact it uses an electric spiral lift instead of the traditional chain to pull vehicles to the highest point, 45 feet in the air. Riders sit in single file, up to six people for a total capacity of 900 riders per hour. Setpoint (just up the road in Ogden, Utah) built and installed a new control system in 1998.

Electric spiral lifts are special in that the vehicles themselves contain small electric traction motors to pull the trains up the hill. The cars engage with an electrified rail on the center of the lift track that provides power to the motors. To keep the weight down the motors have to be small so it is impractical to climb steep lifts, thus the lifts of this type are in an upward spiraling helix to maximize real estate and minimize the grade of the ascent. This system employs anti-rollback devices just as any other roller coaster and once at the top of the lift the train disengages the electrified rail and gravity takes over. At this point the cars begin to cascade down and around steeply banked spirals at varying angles. Oh, and there's no shoulder or lap bars restraints to hold you in, just good old fashioned physics.

30. X2

Known for: World's First 4th Dimension coaster
Park: Six Flags Magic Mountain
Location: United States
Type: Steel
Opened: 2002
Designer/Manufacturer: Arrow Dynamics
Height (ft): 190
Drop (ft): 215
Speed (mph): 76
Inversions: 2
Video: https://www.youtube.com/watch?v=8WTD0Hc9anw

There's nothing ordinary about X2 at Six Flags Magic Mountain. The seats are cantilevered to either side of the track, just like a wing coaster, but with an extra twist – the seats can rotate 360 degrees. It's like a spin-and-puke carnival ride and a hyper coaster had a lovechild together. The demented designers at Arrow drew up this wicked machine that was later perfected by S&S Worldwide. This controlled spinning or rotation is in a direction that is independent of the track – hence, it is like a fourth dimension. There are two sets of rails – one supports the weight of the vehicles while the other is what makes the seats rotate. The vertical distance or displacement between the two sets of rails controls the rotation of the passengers by transforming linear motion into rotational motion, accomplished via a rack and pinion gear.

Here's how it works: The pinion, a typical circular gear, engages the teeth on a linear gear bar (also known as a rack). Thus, as the spacing between the rails changes, the wheels connected to the rack move vertically up or down, causing the pinion gear (or gears) to rotate, flipping the seats as much as 720 degrees. Pushing the rack up cause the seats to spin in one direction whereas pulling the rack down causes the seats to flip in the opposite direction. The amount of rotation is proportional to the displacement between the two sets of rails. No separate power supply is required; the forward motion of the vehicle due to gravity is enough. The pinion gear may actually use a complete gearbox in order to achieve the perfect ratio of linear to rotational motion. Of course, it's not as simple as it sounds because there has to be flexibility built into the system due to vibrations and imperfections in the manufacture of the rails.

With its 360-degree rotating seats and head-first, face down drops, X2 is easily one of the most intense thrill rides on the planet. Riders depart the station facing backwards thus the long climb up the hill is quite agonizing. Let's just get this over with! Before long the top of the hill is reached and after a small dip the seats rotate forward bringing you around to face the ground 200 feet below you. You drop face first, straight down before rotating onto your back midway through the drop, the heavy g-forces pushing you into the seat. After the first drop, the train enters an inside raven loop. As it exits the loop, the seats rotate, executing a lie-to-fly maneuver, transitioning the riders from lying on their backs above the track facing backwards to a flying position hanging under the track facing forward. Shortly after exiting the first vertical turn and while still in the flying position, the seats do a 360 degree rotation backwards, completing a full backflip. Just when you think you can't take anymore, X2 negotiates it's most demented inversion - the half-half - a unique half-twist/forward flip where the track does a 180 roll while the seats perform half a rotation. Another raven turn leads into a fly-to-lie maneuver that transitions the train back on top of the track and the riders onto their backs, looking backward again. Just as soon as you get your bearings, giant flame throwers spit fire overhead, leaving you in awe.

No matter how many coaster notches on your belt, you've never experienced anything quite like X2 – maybe the most terrifying roller coaster you can ride today.

29. MAXIMUM RPM
Known for: Ferris wheel lift
Park: Hard Rock Park
Location: United States
Type: Steel
Opened: 2008
Closed: 2009
Designer/Manufacturer: Premier Rides
Height (ft): 50
Speed (mph): 40.53
Video: https://www.youtube.com/watch?v=BonP23V4gZg

Roller coasters are all about kinetic energy, the energy of movement, versus potential energy, the energy of position. They use stored mechanical energy rather than an engine to operate. As a vehicle travels downhill it trades its "head" or elevation (think of it as the currency of potential energy) for velocity (the currency of kinetic energy). The maximum speed of a coaster is usually achieved in one of two ways: it is lifted to the top of the highest point of the track by a system and then released or it utilizes a mechanism to shoot or launch the vehicle from a standstill to its maximum velocity. In either method, stored energy is converted to active energy.

Maximum RPM, a Premier Rides coaster that operated at the now defunct Hard Rock Park, had probably the most unusual method for a coaster to gain its maximum potential energy. Ladies and gentlemen, behold the Ferris wheel lift. Yes, a Ferris wheel, the popular attraction found at almost every amusement park was used to lift the convertible-styled cars to the highest point. A single car was rolled out of the station and onto a short piece of track attached to a rotatable ring fixed to the inside of a Ferris wheel. The Ferris wheel would complete half a rotation while the track segment stayed upright the entire time thanks to the rotatable ring. After reaching the apex the car would be pushed off at the top into a high speed coaster circuit before returning to the station. Maximum RPM has been standing but not operating (SBNO) for years (since Hard Rock Park, then Freestyle Music Park closed) but has since been taken apart. We may see it pop up at a new home in Vietnam soon.

28. SPIRAL COASTER

Known for: True heartline coaster
Park: Al-Sha'ab Leisure Park
Location: Kuwait
Type: Steel
Opened: 1996
Closed: 2005
Designer/Manufacturer: Intamin
Height (ft): 20
Inversions: 4

The Spiral Coaster at Al-Sha'ab Leisure Park in Kuwait is a true heartline roller coaster. What is the heartline? To keep forces on the riders under acceptable safety limits imposed by ASTM standards, modern roller coasters are designed around the heartline; the average position of all the passenger's hearts. The track should be rotated around the center line or "heartline" of the passengers which lies roughly just above the center of a human torso, above the rails. Roller coasters are all about producing safe accelerations.

Togo and Arrow Dynamics each attempted to make a pipeline coaster where the rails are located on either side of the heartline, in the center of the passengers, rather than above or below them. Intamin's take on this concept began life in 1996 as the Sky Plaza Comet at Lotte Sky Plaza and was indoors. Spiral Coasted was moved outdoors to Al-Sha'ab Leisure Park and renamed The Spiral Coaster. After operating for five years, it closed in 2005 and has been SBNO ever since. Spiral Coaster was rather unique in that there was no lift hill or launch track, because it was partially powered by drive tires. The eight car trains holding two people per car twisted through 1,148 feet of track and four inversions.

27. TULIREKI

Known for: Only operating Mack e-motion coaster
Park: Linnanmäki
Location: Finland
Type: Steel
Opened: 2004
Designer/Manufacturer: Mack Rides
Height (ft): 54.2
Speed (mph): 36
Video: https://www.youtube.com/watch?v=rcm7fsaIMio

For the 27th coaster on our list, we travel to Linnanmäki in Finland, home to two unique roller coasters. Tulireki (which translates to "fire toboggan") is the prototype for the Mack e-motion coaster, the same type as Reaper: Drop Ride to Doom and the only operating one. As with Reaper, the chassis can undulate from side to side, giving the feeling of being dumped out of the vehicle. The trip up the fifty-four foot lift hill leads immediately into some wild mouse style horizontal curves with zero banking. The six passenger car zips through a block brake then curves left into the biggest drop of the ride. More twisting and turning action follows. Another flat block brake passes by before the final two banked curves.

Why have only two e-motion coasters been built? One reason could be capacity; with only single vehicles carrying just six passengers the through-put is low. Another is the swaying action isn't quite enough to make the ride feel truly special. Many riders describe the tilting action as minimal at best. The layouts of the two e-motion coasters are quite similar to a spinning coaster model, and the spinning seats add more thrill than the slight swaying action.

26. STAR JET

Known for: Standup and backwards sitdown trains on one track
Park: Washuzan Highland
Location: Japan
Type: Steel
Opened: 1986
Designer/Manufacturer: Togo
Inversions: 1
Video: https://www.youtube.com/watch?v=JUsGEu0DTCo

The Star Jet at Washuzan Highland has two loading platforms, two queue lines and one track. A backwards traveling sit-down train stops at one platform called the "Backnanger" (an attempt of using both English and Japanese to say "It's backwards!") and a standup train stops at the other platform and is aptly dubbed the "Standing Coaster." The layout of the white tracked coaster is very similar to the former Skyrider at Canada's Wonderland and King Cobra at Kings Island – both proper standup coasters. After a right-hand turn off the lift, the track drops down and into the coaster's single inversion, a tight vertical loop. Next, a rise into a hill leads into a downward spiraling helix. The track then makes a victory lap around the entire circuit with a few random bunny hops thrown in. Star Jet can be classified as one of the twenty-one stand-up coasters built between 1982 and 1999 and may have started the standing coaster fad.

25. WINJAS

Known for: Trick track elements
Park: Phantasialand
Location: Germany
Type: Steel
Opened: 2002
Designer/Manufacturer: Maurer Söhne
Height (ft): 57.08
Speed (mph): 41
Video: https://www.youtube.com/watch?v=vmCXa_HBAFY

Winjas: Force and Fear is a pair of beautifully themed spinning coasters at Phantasialand. Completely enclosed in the fictitious underground civilization of Wuze Town, Winjas dives through statues and set pieces and winds around a large atrium. The unique tracks are each around 1,400 feet in length with a top speed of forty mile per hour. Since 2002, Winjas has been catching unsuspecting riders off guard with its unique trick track elements. The coasters utilize elevator lifts where the track tilts forward at the top of the lift. A set of block brakes on each ride is a section of trick track: one tilts forwards and backwards while the other tilts from side to side. Just when you think the ride is over, the final surprise is a drop track where just prior to the unloading station the track suddenly drops, let's the car pass into the station, before rising back up again. It's the perfect climax to the experience of large drops, hairpin turns, and elaborate theming. Of all the spinning coasters in the world, Winjas just may be the best.

24. BIG GRIZZLY MOUNTAIN
Known for: Lift, backwards drop, and launch
Park: Hong Kong Disneyland
Location: Hong Kong
Type: Steel
Opened: 2012
Designer/Manufacturer: Vekoma
Speed (mph): 56
Video: https://www.youtube.com/watch?v=iCH55433lbI

Big Grizzly Mountain is the latest addition to Disney's mountain range and it's like the Imagineers took the best elements from their most popular attractions - Big Thunder Mountain, Space Mountain, Expedition Everest - and combined them into one exhilarating ride. Centerpiece of the Grizzly Gulch expansion area at Hong Kong Disneyland, the mountain itself is 88 feet tall and resembles the head of a bear (as well as Grizzly Peak at Disney California Adventure). There are enough special effects that it could get nominated for that category in next year's Oscars.

After park goers board the mine train, the coaster begins

gently with a few low speed curves. The first vertical ascent is a simple lift hill found on any other coaster. It's not until we reach the second lift when we start to realize what we're on is truly special. As we're chugging up the second lift, all seems good and well when suddenly a tearing sound is heard, like cables snapping apart. Next thing you know, we're rolling backwards down the lift hill! We panic as we steam backwards, waiting for big crash. But it never happens. A piece of track secretly switched behind us and now we're rolling along a new path. We jog up and down hills unexpectedly as we have no idea what's coming up next.

Finally, we begin to lose steam and back into a shed. Overhead an animatronic bear appears. But wait! Those boxes are labeled TNT. The bear accidently sets off an explosion and in a cloud of fog we rocket forward. A track was switched while we were distracted by the grizzly bear so we're now tearing down an entirely new path. A progression of hills and valleys leads us into a high speed helix before finally slowing down and entering the station.

Big Grizzly Mountain is the second Disney roller coaster to have a backwards section on it (the first being Expedition Everest in Disney's Animal Kingdom). The addition of this superb attraction help propel Hong Kong Disneyland from a second rate park into a top-notch Disney destination.

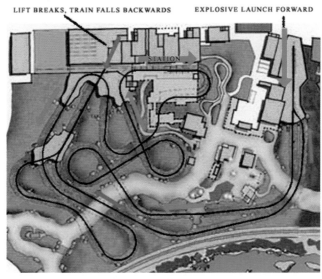

LIFT BREAKS, TRAIN FALLS BACKWARDS   EXPLOSIVE LAUNCH FORWARD

23. TORNADO
Known for: Lift launch spinning coaster
Park: Bakken
Location: Denmark
Type: Steel
Opened: 2009
Designer/Manufacturer: Intamin
Height (ft): 33
Speed (mph): 37
Video: https://www.youtube.com/watch?v=iLtkX5PvXVQ

Yes, there are plenty of spinning coasters out there (like Veil of Dark, Euro Mir, and Winjas on our list) but none of them can match Tornado for its craziness and intensity. Bakken's hair-raising scream machine twists in, around, and through a building as if it were the Tasmanian Devil. Even without the spinning element, Tornado would be an intense ride but Bakken decided to take it to another level and cranked up the vomit meter to eleven. Unlike other spinners, the spinning begins here right from the get go - not halfway through the course. The vehicles feature four seats that all face each other, so you can watch your friend's faces turn green. After the over-the-shoulder restraints are closed and checked, the car is pushed into a left hand turn and the spinning locking mechanism is released. If the ride ops are sadistic they may immediately put your car into a spin. Oh, please no, have mercy on us!

Tornado is compressed into a rather small area. To help save space, Bakken devised the diabolical creation now known as a "lift-launch." Instead of having to build a very tall and land eating lift hill, on the last few feet of Tornado's double-chain lift, the hydraulic motors kick in and accelerate the vehicle to top speed. The boost has the same kick and intensity of a launch coaster and propels the swirling cars into the vortex of tight turns and quick transitions. The trip is extremely disorienting; even trying to describe the layout makes my head hurt. But before you know it you'll be back in the station, quivering like a bowl full of Jell-O. Well done, Bakken, well done indeed.

22. GOLIATH
Known for: Extreme wooden coaster
Park: Six Flags Great America
Location: United States
Type: Wood
Opened: 2014
Designer/Manufacturer: Rocky Mountain Construction
Height (ft): 165
Drop (ft): 180
Speed (mph): 72
Inversions: 2
Video: https://www.youtube.com/watch?v=7SALgjReEiU

Rocky Mountain Construction's second "made from scratch" coaster is the triple world-recording breaking wood coaster Goliath at Six Flags Great America. While a relatively short ride, Outlaw Run's younger but larger sibling is unrelenting from the moment it leaves the lift chain until it pounds into the brake run. Rocky Mountain Construction's new trains for Goliath are very comfortable and you'll be thankful for the seat belt and lap bar when you're hanging upside down. The arched steel support lift hill stands a towering 165 feet. A tunnel at the bottom of the first drop brings the total drop height to 180 feet where you'll hit a blistering 72 miles per hour. On a wooden track no less.

Rocketing out of the tunnel, the overbank turn may not invert as much as some of the other elements on the coaster, but you'll swear you're upside down when maneuvering the turn. The negative-g floater hill following the overbanked turn provides violent-but-amazing airtime. Say goodbye to any loose articles that you should have left in the station or with a non-rider. Next, riders flip head-over-heels through a winding inverted drop similar to a dive loop.

The iconic and lasting image of Goliath is the element hung beneath the lift hill and is known as a zero-g stall. The best way to describe it is like a camel back hill on any other coaster only you're upside down for 80% of it. It's an element that must be experienced to fully understand. Never before have you hung upside down on a roller coaster, at least not for the duration you will on Goliath. While it may not be the longest coaster at Six Flags Great America, it certainly makes every foot of track count.

Not everyone agrees Goliath should be labeled as a wood coaster A typical wood coaster's track consists of a stack of eight pieces of wood, "the stack" being what defines it as a true wooden coaster. The top two pieces of wood are wider than the stack they sit on so the safety or up-stop wheels can run below them thus preventing the vehicles from leaving the track. Rocky Mountain Construction has developed a new technology called "topper track" where the top two pieces of a wood coaster's stack are replaced with steel and filled with a high strength concrete grout. In fact, the ride becomes so smooth that enthusiasts argue that these are no longer wooden roller coasters and should be classified as something entirely different. Combine this with that fact that the lift hill's structure is composed of steel, and many coaster enthusiasts think Goliath should be classified as a new category of ride: the hybrid. Whatever you want to classify it, Goliath is epic in every sense of the word.

21. EUROMIR
Known for: Unique spinning coaster
Park: Europa Park
Location: Germany
Type: Steel
Opened: 1997
Designer/Manufacturer: Mack Rides
Height (ft): 92
Speed (mph): 49.7
Video: https://www.youtube.com/watch?v=PpxgVVeWu4M

If there's one thing you should know about Europe, it's that they know how to turn everything into a party. And roller coasters are no exception. Stationed in Germany's Europa Park, EuroMir is an exciting recreation of Russian space missions. Riders are seated back-to-back in four person spinning cars. Yeah, you read that right. Each circular car spins at different points throughout the one-of-a-kind ride. In fact, EuroMir was one of the first spinning coasters, but unlike most of its kin, the spinning is controlled by motors and not physics.

The ride begins close to ground level as the cars enter a tower filled with upbeat dance tunes and flashing lights, which is really a spiral lift to the top. This elevation is meant to act like riders are going into space and lasts around two minutes, so riders can have a little dance party as they spin past astronauts and machines replicating the Russian space station, Mir. Once they reach the top, they "re-enter" Earth's atmosphere and are sent out of the tower, still spinning slowly around each of three mirrored towers. After "orbiting" around, the cars lock and the real "re-entry" begins. They suddenly drop down 86 feet and continue to be thrown around turns and into drops until they are at ground level again. So the ride may start off slow and spinney, but it picks up so quickly in the final portion that it shocks you out of the trance you were put in by the sweet music. Just hope you aren't the one facing backwards through the drops. The only thing more intense than sudden drops are sudden drops that everyone sees coming but you. Or maybe that's what makes this ride so popular.

20. WILD MOUSE
Known for: Wooden wild mouse coaster
Park: Blackpool
Location: United Kingdom
Type: Wood
Opened: 1958
Designer/Manufacturer: Frank Wright/ Pleasure Beach Blackpool
Height (ft): 50
Speed (mph): 35
Video: https://www.youtube.com/watch?v=8VojCzmGyB0

There it sits, as quiet as a mouse, dwarfed by the surrounding steel behemoth's like Pepsi Max Big One. Despite its deceptive appearance, Blackpool's first major attraction built after World War II is one of the most extreme roller coasters around. Wild Mouse is only one of five wooden wild mouse style coasters left in the world. It's the ancestor for an entire breed of modern steel coasters and yet it may pack more intensity per square foot than any modern equivalent.

As with most wild mouse coasters, the wheels are positioned towards the rear of the car, creating the illusion that you are about to fly off the track at every horizontal turn. The mouse faces on the front of the cars seem so innocent but beware; this rodent has a bite. The track is crammed into more-or-less of a cube, minus one turn that pops out over the top of the extended queue. The lethal hairpin turns are taken at an unbelievable speed. Riders will tremble and flop like rag dolls as they're thrown around over the surprising airtime filled drops.

Wild Mouse certainly has a reputation. If you search the internet for reviews you'll read comments that may sound similar to: "If you come off without a mild case of whiplash and at least a dozen bruises then you haven't ridden it right." "Battered and bruised, you come off smiling - a proper experience." "Best vintage ride in the park, brutal and tummy tickling, they don't or won't ever make rides like this ever again." "This must be the world's most violent theme park ride still standing. But I love it - a hearty 'up yours' to Health & Safety." If you want to brave the Wild Mouse, you might want to do so soon. Rumors about the legendary ride's potential demise have been swirling, claiming Blackpool may be forced to close the classic due to safety reasons.

19. DAIDARASAURUS

Known for: Mobius roller coaster
Park: Expoland
Location: Japan
Opened: 1970
Closed: 2007
Designer/Manufacturer: Sansei Technologies
Height (ft): 92
Speed (mph): 45
Video: https://www.youtube.com/watch?v=vJXe9pC9V7I

Osaka, Japan was once home to Expoland, an amusement park that thrived for over thirty years. The park was initially planned as a temporary installation for the International Exposition in 1970 (Expo '70). Closed immediately following Expo '70, the popularity of the park lead to its re-opening on March 15, 1972. The star attraction of Expoland was the colossal coaster known as Daidarasaurus. This steel beast began prowling the park as a dueling/racing coaster with two separate tracks. . The white, latticed steel supported long, drawn out hills. When watching videos of the coaster in action it almost looks like it is traveling in slow motion.

In 1999, the two sides were combined to make one outrageously long track, referred to as a Mobius coaster. Adding the two tracks together resulted in Daidarasaurus becoming the second longest roller coaster in the world behind Steel Dragon 2000. That is, if you counted it as one ride as there would be countless disputes about the ride's record length.

Daidarasaurus is now extinct. On May 5, 2007, a 19-year-old university student was killed and nineteen other guests were injured when another coaster at the park, Fujin Rajin II, derailed due to a broken axle. None of the ride vehicle's axles had been replaced for fifteen years. The park reopened after the accident but closed again on December 9, 2007, citing a lack of customers. On February 9, 2009, its owners finally decided that the park was closed down for good and Daidarasaurus was torn down.

18. THE ULTIMATE

Known for: Long terrain coaster
Park: Lightwater Valley
Location: United Kingdom
Type: Steel
Opened: 1991
Designer/Manufacturer: Big Country Motioneering & British Rail
Height (ft): 107
Speed (mph): 51
Video: https://www.youtube.com/watch?v=ioaBUnHDSyk

Opened in 1991, this tubular steel coaster is currently the second longest roller coaster in the world at 7,442 feet (behind Steel Dragon 2000). The seven and a half minute ride sprawls over 44 acres of beautiful English countryside. The best way to describe the Ultimate may be to call it the steel, European version of the infamous Beast at Kings Island, the only two members of the 7,000 foot club. The Ultimate's two lift hills are 102 and 107 feet tall respectively and result in the ride having a top speed of 51 miles per hour. Those lifts are really the only visible features of the half-wood half-steel supported coaster. Lightwater Valley was blessed with uneven topography and thank goodness the designers had the twisted imagination to take advantage of it. The ride's profile contours to the rolling knolls and valleys of the wooded country side, generating increased drama as the upcoming track lies hidden behind the next green hill. The never-ending turns have you smashed against the walls of the car. In fact, some of the banked turns had to re-engineered to reduce the forces on the passengers and the vehicles.

The Ultimate has become world famous for more than just being an endurance test. It was recreated as "The Storm" in the Katie's World scenario in the original RollerCoaster Tycoon simulator game. The Ultimate also made headlines for two separate incidents of the train colliding with a deer on the tracks. Only one person was injured in both accidents, though the deer did not survive. As with any modern roller coaster, all the low points in the ride are fenced off for safety but occasionally an animal will sneak in.

17. LOST COASTER

Known for: Vertical lift, tight turn radii
Park: Indiana Beach
Location: United States
Type: Wood
Opened: 2002
Designer/Manufacturer: Custom Coasters International
Height (ft): 35
Speed (mph): 20
Video: https://www.youtube.com/watch?v=WmRMwy3-cnk

For the next coaster on the list, we visit the small lakeside park, Indiana Beach in Monticello, Indiana for one of the most unique wooden coasters ever built. What is possibly one of the longest names for a coaster, The Lost Coaster of Superstition Mountain began as a small mine themed powered dark ride, but in 2002, it was completely renovated by Custom Coasters Inc (CCI) to become the compact coaster it is today. This was also the last project CCI fully completed before they went under later that year.

Lost Coaster uses custom made two-car trains by CCI that can turn on a dime. The curves may have the tightest radius on any roller coaster ever. Each car holds up to four passengers that sit facing inwards. A vertical elevator lift takes the vehicles to the top of the "mountain" before depositing them into the caverns of surprising turns and sudden drops. The ride does feel like an out of control mine train with sharp bends and oddly banked track as you're taken around in and out of the mountain. Lost Coaster is also significant in that it was the first wooden coaster to use magnetic brakes. It's not easy to get to, Indiana Beach being in the middle of nowhere, but the trek is worth it to experience this quirky little ride.

16. VONKAPUTOUS

Known for: Water coaster
Park: Linnanmäki
Location: Finland
Type: Steel
Opened: 2001
Designer/Manufacturer: Premier Rides
Height (ft): 79
Speed (mph): 37.3
Video: https://www.youtube.com/watch?v=uyglYXMXnic

Vonkaputous is one of two liquid coasters produced by American company Premier Rides and is the only remaining one in the world today. Themed to Finnish lumberjack and sawmills, the carved-out-log looking vehicles depart the station and quickly ascend the 79 foot tall lift hill. The view is fleeting as the cars take a steep dive to the right and crash through a fog filled building. The track twists up and to the right, followed by a brief straightaway. With bated breath, we brace ourselves for the epic finale. The track drops down to the left and plunges into an icy pool of water, drenching us to our bones. The vehicles never leave the steel track so the current carries us back to the loading station. The waterline in the splash down pool is monitored constantly: too low and the deceleration will not be enough to safely slow the vehicles. Vonkaputous's top speed of 37 miles per hour and simple figure eight layout of just over 1,000 feet of track look meager on paper, but the final drop and splash down make it a ride to remember.

15. G-FORCE
Known for: Inverted lift hill
Park: Drayton Manor
Location: United Kingdom
Type: Steel
Opened: 2005
Designer/Manufacturer: Maurer Söhne
Height (ft): 82
Speed (mph): 43.5
Inversions: 3
Video: http://www.youtube.com/watch?v=sDibFwuWHPE

G-Force was only the second Maurer Söhne X-Car coaster to be built in the world (the first being the prototype Sky Wheel at Skyline Park in Germany). Drayton Manor's new, state-of-the-art roller coaster features wide-open X-Car trains, lap bars (remember that), and a capacity of 1,000 people an hour. The most terrifying feature of G-Force is the humpty-bump lift hill where terrified riders are pulled up the first half of a vertical loop until they are

completely inverted. And, yes, inverted means upside down. You'll be begging for mercy and the ride has barely begun. After being released from the weird lift the inverted vehicles swoop down, finish the loop, reach a speed of 40 mph, and complete the rest of the coaster's twisted circuit, including a unique double inversion known as a bent Cuban eight. It's another small, compact layout but it throws quite the punch!

14. STEEPLECHASE
Known for: three tracked racing roller coaster
Park: Blackpool
Location: United Kingdom
Type: Steel
Opened: 1977
Designer/Manufacturer: Arrow Dynamics
Video: https://www.youtube.com/watch?v=GHxOr65xa-w

Steeplechase is not only the name of the next coaster on our list but it's also the name for the style of coaster. The classic

steeplechase roller coaster is known for its horse-shaped vehicles and side-by-side track arrangements that leads to wild racing and dueling elements. Some steeplechase coasters, like the one that existed at Kennywood, had as many as six tracks. The thrills come from the racing rather than the size of the drops. Steeplechase coasters have all but disappeared due to large space requirements, low capacity, low thrill factor, and today's strict safety standards.

Custom designed by Arrow Dynamics and opened in 1977, Blackpool's is the only operating steeplechase style roller coaster left in the world. One or two riders straddle the horse-shaped vehicle on one of three parallel tracks. The fiberglass steeds' front grab rail is rather low, so you'll be forced to adopt the jockey riding position. The layout unfurls in a twisted figure eight with two chain lift hills along the way. The triplet tracks wind around and underneath the classic Big Dipper and Nickelodeon Streak coasters. The new jockeys will negotiate a grassy obstacle course, leaping over fences and gliding around turns. Blackpool should be applauded for keeping this historically significant ride operating. So take the reins, hold on tight, and enjoy the race.

13. LEAP THE DIPS

Known for: Side Friction
Park: Lakemont Park
Location: United States
Type: Wood
Opened: 1902
Designer/Manufacturer: Edward Joy Morris Company
Height (ft): 41
Drop (ft): 9
Speed (mph): 18
Video: https://www.youtube.com/watch?v=--64I9gH9DU

A little park in Altoona, Pennsylvania is home to the oldest operating coaster in the world. Lakemont Park built Leap the Dips in 1902 and while it is the oldest operating now, it actually closed in 1985 due to disrepair. A fund-raising campaign led to a restoration starting in 1997 and a reopening on Memorial Day 1999. Therefore, the oldest *continually*-operating roller coaster is the 1911 built Scenic Railway at Luna Park in Melbourne, Australia.

There's a saying in the amusement industry, "you never stop building a wooden coaster." On average, every piece of wood in the support structure will be replaced at least once every seven years. So, how much of the original structure of Leap the Dips is left is hard to say, though that has not prevented it from being added to the National Register of Historic Places and designated a National Historic Landmark. It is also an American Coaster Enthusiasts Coaster Classic and Coaster Landmark□.

Once very common, Leap the Dips is one of the only remaining side friction roller coasters still operating. Side mounted wheels on the coaster cars ride against side fraction rails which are perpendicular to the load carrying rails. The main, horizontal rails support the weight of the vehicle while the side rails guide it through the course. A side friction roller coaster has no upstop wheels so there is no way to prevent the cars from lifting off of the track. Rides can be rough due to the amount of play between the friction wheels and guide track.

Leap the Dips is quite tame compared to today's standards. The maximum height is an unimpressive 41 feet and the average speed a measly ten miles per hour. The double figure eight layout features mainly near horizontal track punctuated by a few small, well, dips. It's a true blast from the past.

12. DIVERTICAL
Known for: Water coaster with elevator lift
Park: Mirabilandia
Location: Italy
Type: Steel
Opened: 2012
Designer/Manufacturer: Intamin
Height (ft): 197
Speed (mph): 65
Video: https://www.youtube.com/watch?v=cHxqNFut2d8

Divertical is the next generation of Intamin water coaster. Outside of the station, the journey begins and ends as a boat ride, floating through a U-shaped channel. After securing the over-the-shoulder lap bars, the coaster boats gently drop down into the water and proceed to slowly bob through the cement trough, giving riders more than enough time to appreciate the 197 foot tall open air elevator looming ever closer. Gazing up at the monstrous bow legged supports does make one pause and question their decision to ride. As your vehicle scoots forward onto the elevator platform transitioning from boat to coaster, I dare you to look straight up. The lift begins straight up, but as you approached the bowed out segment in the middle you tilt to the outside followed by tilting to the inside.

You only have a second to admire the view before you're plummeting downward. While the descent isn't steep, the nearly 200 foot tall drop seems to last forever. We rocket down a straightaway skirting over water before going up and over an airtime filler camelback hill. We're slammed into a hard banked left hand turn, skid over a mid-course brake run without slowing down, then flow with feverish fluidity in a downward spiraling helix. A final drop and we fall into the waiting pool, a torrent of water splashing over the sides of the boat. Whoa! We float quickly back to the station, unload, dry off, and get right back in line. The 197 foot drop is enormous for a water ride, it's the trip to the top that will give anxiety and be implanted in your brain forever.

11. RUTSCHEBANEN
Known for: Brakeman
Park: Tivoli Gardens
Location: Denmark
Type: Wood
Opened: 1914
Designer/Manufacturer: Valdemar Lebech
Height (ft): 39.3
Speed (mph): 31.1
Video: https://www.youtube.com/watch?v=P3Gv3QomoQg

Rutschebanen (or "Roller Coaster") is a scenic railway roller coaster at Tivoli Gardens in Copenhagen, Sjælland, Denmark. The ride was built by the famous LaMarcus A. Thompson in 1914. It is a "side friction" roller coaster, so the trains are not locked on the track. One of the very few scenic railways left in the world still operated by a brakeman. Yes, a brakeman (or brake woman) rides on the two by twelve trains and controls the speed of the ride by applying a hand brake when necessary. There are no brakes mounted to the tracks as modern coasters operate. The 2,362 feet of track weaves in and around a themed mountain at a top speed of 31 mph and a height of 43 feet. This classic coaster is the third oldest roller coaster in operation.

10. ATLANTIS ADVENTURE
Known for: Aqua trax
Park: Lotte World
Location: South Korea
Type: Steel
Opened: 2003
Designer/Manufacturer: Intamin
Height (ft): 72.2
Speed (mph): 46.6
Video: https://www.youtube.com/watch?v=074Ttd1a4OM

Atlantis Adventure marked the debut of a new style of roller coaster, the Aqua Trax. Developed by Intamin, Aqua Trax is a family thrill type roller coaster featuring water effects and elements. Central to this concept is the revolutionary new vehicle, designed so that the guests will sit astride, like on a motorcycle or a jet ski rather than inside a boat usually seen in a water ride. It uses a new restraint system over the laps, allowing freedom for riders' upper body. In this way, they will feel much more part of the ride and not just a passive spectator. Furthermore, the seating is staggered in height.

The eight passenger vehicles are launched via LIMs into a 72 foot tall top hat element fully enclosed inside the Atlantis themed building. Next, you catch a glimmer of sunlight as you briefly twist around outside before darting back into the building. This action repeats a few times before we take a large drop down over a pool. The cars follow the track as it makes an S-curve inches above the waterline, a maneuver that has us feeling like we're really catching some waves on the back of a jet ski. But the moment ends all too soon and we hit the brakes. Aw man, it's over already? Not quite!

A U-shaped turn through the bowels of the ruins includes an encounter with a plant/dragon looking thing. We survive only to arrive at the base of a lift hill looking track, only it's powered by LIMs and not chains. Up and away we go. Once we reach the apex, the view is fleeting as we're whisked around a 180 degree elevated turn before the bottom drops out. A quick trip around and through the building again before we arrive at another pool. We skim across it like a skipping rock before hitting the final brake run. Whee! Can we do that again?

9. SKYTRAK

Known for: World's first "flying" coaster
Park: Granada Studios
Location: United Kingdom
Type: Steel
Opened: 1997
Closed: 1998
Designer/Manufacturer: Skytrak International
Height (ft): 50
Speed (mph): 28

"It's a bird! It's a plane! It's Superman!" That's what visitors to Granada Studios were exclaiming in 1997 as they witnessed other humans soaring over their heads. Contrary to popular beliefs, Skytrak was the world's first "flying" roller coaster – a type of coaster where passengers lie prone with their bodies being parallel to the track. Designed and built by Skytrak International, a subsidiary of Fairpoint Engineering, nobody had ever seen or experienced anything like Skytrak before. To board the torture-device looking vehicle was almost like climbing a ladder, very similar to the Volare flying coasters built by Zamperla today. The single rail track twisted above Granada Studios in several large turns, spiraling helixes, and small bunny hops.

The experience of flying solo was unique but at a cost to the ride's throughput (THRC), with only one rider per car and only five cars could operate at once, though rarely did. The ride was plagued with mechanical issues including a derailment during a test run. The £1 million investment closed in 1998, immediately dismantled and scrapped. The park itself ran into financial problems and ended up closing the same year. The next flying coaster, and first successful one, was Stealth at Paramount's Great America, designed by Vekoma (currently called Nighthawk and resides at Carowinds).

8. MILKY WAY
Known for: Sitdown vs. Standup dual coaster
Park: Mitsui Greenland
Location: Japan
Type: Steel
Opened: 1991
Designer/Manufacturer: Togo
Height (ft): 125
Video: https://www.youtube.com/watch?v=hHL1FIXJK6U

Milky Way is another unique dueling roller coaster. Originally it was named Ultra Twin and opened in 1991 as part of the Garden and Greenery Expo in Osaka. At an unspecified time it was renamed to Fujin Rajin (not to be confused with Fujin Rajin II at Expoland). In 2007, the ride was renamed a third time to Milky Way.

What makes it unique is the pink side of the Milky Way uses sit-down trains while the blue side has stand-up trains. Originally, both sides had stand-up trains. At various times during the ride, one train is a little ahead of the other, and the track is designed to give several opportunities to pass head-on and ride alongside the other train. The stand-up side has a wicked bunny hop along the ride. One trademark of TOGO's roller coasters is the placement of catwalks running the majority of the track, like on a wood coaster, making it easier for maintenance to do their daily inspections.

7. GRAVITY MAX

Known for: World's only tilt coaster
Park: Lihpao Land
Location: Taiwan
Type: Steel
Opened: 2002
Designer/Manufacturer: Vekoma
Height (ft): 114
Speed (mph): 56
Inversions: 1
Video: http://www.youtube.com/watch?v=aA4_BjmHzAM

Gravity Max in Taiwan's Discovery World theme park is the world's only "tilt coaster". The coaster begins innocently enough by ascending a typical chain lift hill. But upon cresting the apex rider's notice the track suddenly ends! The rails stop and there is nothing but blue sky. The train keeps moving until it reaches the end of the track when it thankfully stops. What happens next will blow your mind – the entire section of track the vehicle is now sitting on slowly rotates ninety degrees. We're now staring straight down, our hearts pound like jackhammers inside our chests, and we pray the rails are lined up. The movable segment is locked into the next section of track and without warning the train is released. All the air is sucked out of our lungs as we plummet 114 feet. After the vertical drop into a tunnel, we're subjected to a forceful turn, a vertical loop, and a gut-wrenching helix before returning flummoxed to the station. Those twisted Dutch thrill ride designers at Vekoma had the audacity to build this crazy contraption – the only one like it in the world today and a truly terrifying coaster.

6. ADVENTURE DRIVE
Known for: Scream powered
Park: Suzuka Circuit
Location: Japan
Type: Steel
Opened: 2014
Designer/Manufacturer: Hoei Sangyo Co., Ltd.
Video: https://www.youtube.com/watch?v=fuCQ8dnbVzA

Adventure Drive, one of two roller coasters at Suzuka Circuit in Japan, has introduced a new take on interactive rides. After four brave explorers have climbed into the jeep themed cars, the odd journey begins innocently enough with a few low to the ground turns leading up to a standard chain lift. The lift is short as the entire ride is rather close to the ground so it doesn't take long before they arrive at the first weird feature - another lift but this time it's powered by drive tires rather than a chain. Why? There is no discernible reason for why the manufacturer, Hoei Sangyo Co, choose to use a chain on one lift and tires on the next.

After more turns and tiny drops through Egyptian ruin type theming the car finally arrives at a long straight away where passengers are instructed to scream as loud as they can. The louder the riders scream, the faster they will go in the following launch track. Yes, it's apparently the world's first "scream powered" roller coaster. A microphone mounted above the track picks up the screams and the louder they are the more power is supplied to the cable launch system. If you choose to remain quiet you'll still launch but you won't have as much fun. Just imagine this technology implemented on a much larger coaster.

5. REVERSER

Known for: Backwards "spin-about" track switches
Park: Saltair
Location: United States
Type: Wood
Opened: 1915
Closed: 1925
Designer/Manufacturer: Frank F. Hoover / Thomas Hooper
Video (RollerCoaster Tycoon example):
 https://www.youtube.com/watch?v=r1yVVrfHddg

The popular RollerCoaster Tycoon computer game featured a unique type of coaster you could build called the "wooden reverser roller coaster." Nothing similar to this exists today leading many to assume the wooden reverser was imagined specifically for the game. However, this type of coaster is historically accurate and at least one actually did exist. The Reverser (or Hooper Reverser) was a real roller coaster that thrilled riders during the 1920s. Reverser could be found at Saltair, an amusement park built on a huge fill on the Great Salt Lake west of Salt Lake City Utah. Not much is known about this unusual contraption invented by Thomas Hooper and designed by Frank F. Hoover. In his book "*The Incredible Scream Machine: A History of the Roller Coaster*" Robert Cartmell writes the following: "It was a straightforward legitimate roller coaster until the rear wheels swiveled out and around on tracks of their own. Passengers then rode sections backward until the next spin-about. Riders were never sure which way they would face during the run since there were several turning points." Sadly, the Reverser met its demise in a 1925 fire and burned to the ground.

Essentially this coaster used a variation of the side friction track where there are no up-stop wheels on the underside of the track to prevent it from falling off. There would be two sets of track. One for the front wheels, one for the back, offset just a bit. One set of wheels stay straight while another set of wheels on bearings travels on a branch track, causing the vehicle to pivot about the first set of wheels. This would cause the front of the car to whip around, and be pulled by the back. To bring the car back forward, it would do the same thing, but with the back (now running in front) wheels first.

To get a better idea, see the images in Hooper's patent:

https://www.google.com/patents/US1508453?dq=Hooper+Amusement+apparatus&hl=en&sa=X&ei=ObPHVOKYKI_3yQT3hIHoCg&ved=0CCQQ6AEwAQ

4. FLYING TURNS

Known for: Wooden bobsled coaster
Park: Knoebels
Location: United States
Type: Wood
Opened: 2013
Designer/Manufacturer: Knoebels Amusement Resort
Height (ft): 50
Speed (mph): 24
Video: https://www.youtube.com/watch?v=EhssEESfT5I

Visitors to amusement parks throughout the 1930s and 40s were terrorized by a unique style of coaster - the flying turns. The flying turns style ride is essentially like a bobsled found in the Winter Olympics only it runs on wheels and wood instead of blades and ice. The trains were free to roll around the trough so subsequent rides may not take the exact same path through the  course. The Lake Placid Bobsled built for Palisades Park, New Jersey in 1937, was considered the fiercest flying turns style coaster. As with most of the turns, it only lasted a mere nine years when it was dismantled in 1946 due to low ridership, rider complaints, and mounting maintenance costs. The wooden bobsled fell out of favor, the last closing in 1974, and modern bobsleds were built out of more durable steel and fiberglass.

That is until a little park in Pennsylvania decided to attempt the impossible - resurrect the wooden bobsled coaster and make it safe and efficient enough for modern standards. This daunting

challenge almost proved to be too much. This engineeri ng nightmar
e was scheduled to open in 2006 but the park soon discovered it would be harder than originally thought to get the trains to perform as expected. Multiple iterations of the vehicles were tested and modifications were made to the track without success. But the park persisted, kept iterating, brought in the best coaster designers, and after seven years of work, The Flying Turns opened to the public in October, 2013. The result of this labor of love is a 47-foot-tall, 1,200-foot-long ride with three lift hills, a 540-degree helix and a double figure-eight course, the bulk of which is constructed of southern yellow pine. Trains consist of three two-person cars that swoop and swerve as they negotiate the twists and turns. Flying Turns is also one of the rare coasters to contain three lift hills.

Flying Turns is a true hidden gem and Knoebels is probably the only park in the world that could spend seven years developing a ride like this in full view of the public. Thank goodness they accomplished this incredible feat and the ride is open for us all to enjoy.

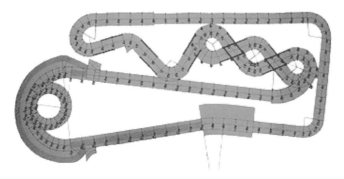

3. GREEN DRAGON
Known for: Powered by people
Park: GreenWood Forest Park
Location: United Kingdom
Type: Steel
Opened: 2004
Designer/Manufacturer: WGH Transportation
Speed (mph): 25
Video: https://www.youtube.com/watch?v=uGlvgzAmCzU

If you travel to Wales in the United Kingdom you'll find one of the most energy efficient roller coasters in the world. The Green Dragon at GreenWood Forest Park is the world's first people-powered roller coaster. It's based on an old fashioned inclined railway system developed for mines and quarries intended to move heavy coal down steep slopes without having any external energy source. Here's how it works:

Riders climb up to the top of a hill level with the coaster's empty station where they board a funicular (or tram). The tram descends the hill on a track under the weight of the passengers. Through a system of cables and pulleys, the empty coaster train (which weighs less than the combined weight of the tram and passengers) is lifted to the top of the hill on a detached section of track. The passengers then disembark the tram at the bottom of the hill and have to climb another walkway back up to the loading station to board the coaster train. The empty track on which the train was sitting uses gravity to descend back down the hill to await the coaster train at the exit platform, pulling the tram back up to the station level in the process. It's all about energy transfer: When the passengers climb to the top of the hill they gain potential energy. As the tram descends the potential energy is converted into kinetic energy to pull the train back up the hill.

As for the ride itself, it's pretty tame, even for a family coaster. Out of the station it starts a meandering descent down the hill side, turning left then right over and over again. The muted green track sticks close to the ground and doesn't really have any straight forward drops. The Green Dragon is a unique "eco-coaster" that forces its riders to get some extra exercise.

2. VERTIGO

Known for: Extreme suspended coaster
Park: Walibi Belgium
Location: Belgium
Type: Steel
Opened: 2007
Closed: 2008
Designer/Manufacturer: Doppelmayr
Height (ft): 180
Speed (mph): 37
Video: https://www.youtube.com/watch?v=cB_U4mm2PGU

Vertigo is a perfect case study for why an amusement park would opt to go with a cloned and proven ride versus trying to create a new, unique type of roller coaster. Walibi Belgium partnered with Doppelmayr, a well-known manufacturer of cable cars, to create what would have been the world's largest suspended style roller coaster. Built in the spring of 2006 and intended to open that season, technical problems delayed the opening of Vertigo to the public until June 14th, 2007. Shortly after, more problems forced the closure of the ride for the rest of the year while the track was taken down and reworked. On May 8th, 2008 the Vertigo had its official opening with fireworks, lots of media, and an appearance by Jean-Claude Van Damme.

Vertigo was a sight to behold - frightening and fascinating at the same time - and unlike any other roller coaster ever built. The 2,369 foot course was supported by what looked like too few futuristic silver towers. The track hung like a loosely attached rope draped between each mast over 180 feet in the air. Designed to resemble a hang glider, the set of four seats was freely suspended under the chassis and could swing from side to side with only a lapbar to keep guests in their seats.

What made Vertigo different from almost every other roller coaster is the lack of brakes on the whole track circuit. Each of the eight vehicles had its own braking system on board. The distances and positions of the vehicles were transmitted and monitored by the ride control system (RCS). In case of a malfunction the vehicle then could brake to a full stop. This happens at certain declined points on the track so that the vehicle can continue the trip and return to the station by its own with no need to power it from outside – which was good news considering large stretches of the course were unsupported with no means to access a stuck vehicle.

After the vertical elevator lift brought you to the 180 foot mark, you were treated to a breathtaking view of the park and beautiful countryside sprawled far below you. After release, the car seemingly floated away as if an invisible hand were guiding it. For those afraid of heights it was pure and simple psychological torture. The leisurely paced trip contained no inversions and had a top speed of 37 miles per hour. Extreme thrill ride Vertigo was not, but the feeble looking structure combined with the height of the ride and only lap bar restraints made a terrifying experience for all.

Unfortunately, more technical problems were encountered and just eleven days later on May 19th, 2008 the Vertigo closed once again. In December of 2008, the removal of the Vertigo was started and demolition was completed during the winter of 2009. In the end, the park deemed the ride would be too expensive to maintain, wasn't reliable, and did not have an acceptable capacity. They tried to build something new, something unique, something the world had never experienced before. And at first this innovative ride system seemed destined to appear at amusement parks and ski resorts all over the world. But in the end the concept proved to be a failure. It was then and likely will always be one of a kind.

1. TRANAN

Known for: Only free fly model ever built
Park: Skara Sommarland
Location: Sweden
Type: Steel
Opened: 2009
Designer/Manufacturer: S&S Worldwide
Height (ft): 65.6
Speed (mph): 24.9
Video: https://www.youtube.com/watch?v=dBIYDmEtEVU

Birds in flight are the physical embodiment of beauty and grace. But what happens when humans want to fly like our feathery friends? They ride Tranan, of course! Located in Sweden's Skara Sommarland, Tranan is literally one *big* bird of a ride. A suspended free fly coaster from S&S, and the only one of its kind, Tranan takes riders under its wings (literally) as it soars through twists and turns.

What makes Tranan unique is may be the oddest roller coaster vehicle you'll ever board. The main body of the vehicle sits above the track and is shaped like a giant X with two canoes hung between the outstretched arms of the car on either side of the track. Each passenger car is situated on either wing of the massive bird, holding four riders each in a single file line. Since it is a free flying coaster, the cars do not stay in place while going through turns, and especially inversions. But riders never actually go upside down while the bird does. Instead, when the bird begins to flip, the cars *rotate*, sending the left above to the right and the right under to the left side. The track twists upside down along with the main body of the vehicle but the two passenger cars stay upright.

Although this ride only reaches speeds of 25 mph and doesn't have any drops or classic inversions, the fact that riders are suspended freely and rock uncontrollably is enough to make this seemingly childish ride intense and fun for anyone. If it's so much fun, why haven't more free fly coasters been sold? The answer is straight forward: low capacity. THRC is a mere 480 to 600 people per hour. At IAAPA, S&S introduced a new twist on the free fly, the

Free Fly X variation with seats facing forwards and backwards. The ride experience features the same longitudinal rotations performed by the Free Fly but with increased capacity.

Unique Coaster Statistics

Where are these one-of-a-kind scream machines located? The majority of unusual roller coasters are found in the United States and Europe, followed by Japan. The complete breakdown by country:

United States: 14	Russia: 1
Japan: 6	Taiwan: 1
United Kingdom: 6	Italy: 1
Germany: 3	Hong Kong: 1
Denmark: 3	Netherlands: 1
Finland: 2	Spain: 1
Australia: 2	Singapore: 1
UAE: 2	Switzerland: 1
Belgium: 1	South Korea: 1
Sweden: 1	Kuwait: 1

There are only three amusement parks that have more than one ride on this list: Six Flags Magic Mountain, Blackpool Pleasure Beach, and Linnanmaki.

Who builds the most unique roller coasters? Interestingly, B&M, considered by many to be the BMW of roller coaster companies, does not manufacture a single coaster on this list, and that may be by design. Conversely, Intamin seems to be the company most willing to take risks and push the envelope. The complete breakdown:

Intamin: 8	Zierer: 2
Vekoma: 4	Gerstlauer: 2
Premier Rides: 4	Arrow Dynamics: 2
Mack Rides: 4	Pax Company: 1
Togo: 3	The Gravity Group: 1
Maurer Söhne: 3	B&M: 0
S&S Worldwide: 2	

Many of these unique roller coasters are prototypes, meaning the first of their type ever built, so it's not surprising to see the average track length of all these coasters is a modest 2,354 feet. Over statistics that may interest only me:

Type
Steel: 42
Wood: 8

Status
Currently operating: 48
Defunct: 12

Features
Number that go upside down: 15 (30%)
Number that go backwards: 7   (14%)
Number that feature a launch segment: 11 (22%)

Narrowly Missed the List

With over 3,000 roller coasters worldwide it's hard to narrow a list down to just fifty. Here's a few other extreme roller coasters considered but in the end did not make the cut:

- ❖ Dauling Dragons, Happy Valley - world's first "high five" element
- ❖ Dragon Challenge, Islands of Adventure – dueling inverted coaster
- ❖ Fantaisa Special, Tongdo Fantasia - world's only triple corkscrew element
- ❖ Orphan Rocker - cool name
- ❖ Powder Keg, Silver Dollar City - compressed air launch and lift hill in the same ride
- ❖ Racer, Kennywood – a Mobius racing coaster
- ❖ Roller Soaker, HersheyPark – rare Setpoint coaster
- ❖ Seven Dwarfs Mine Ride, Magic Kingdom - swaying mine cars
- ❖ The Smiler, Alton Towers - more inversions than any other coaster
- ❖ Ultra Twister, AstroWorld – pipeline coaster

What the Future Holds

Roller coaster designers are constantly innovating and pushing the limits. The roller coasters of tomorrow will look far different than the thrill rides of today. A peek into the near future shows some innovative upcoming coasters will come online:

- ❖ Orlando's Skyscraper will be the world's tallest roller coaster and first over 500 feet.

- ❖ Batman: The Ride at Six Flags Fiesta Texas, will be the first 4D free spin by S&S.

- ❖ Cannibal at Lagoon Park will use an elevator lift followed by the world's steepest drop.

- ❖ Thunderbird at Holiday World is America's first launched wing rider.

- ❖ ZDT's Switchback is a shuttle coaster made out of wood! This Gravity Group woodie will also be the first shuttle coaster with a full chain lift and first drop experience.

- ❖ A Dynamic Attractions multi-direction coaster could be built at Ferrari World which will feature movable track segments.

Enjoy the Ride

Roller coaster fanatics are constantly craving taller, faster, longer, and more intense thrill rides. Upon each visit to the amusement park, the ante must be upped. Parks look to innovate, to one-up their competitors. "World's First" is the most popular marketing strategy today. Theme parks will take financial risks for something no one else in the world has, and the fans will travel from all over to brave it. The challenge for the designers is how to make the experiences ever more extreme while maintaining the same standards for safety?

Roller coasters come in a mind-blowing profusion of styles. Some are successful and will eventually be replicated in the future. Others are unique because, well, the idea wasn't very good. Or too expensive to maintain. Either way, the end of the roller coaster's evolution is, thankfully, nowhere in sight. I look forward to riding the scream machines of the future.

Ride on!

-Nick Weisenberger

Would You Like to Know More About Roller Coaster Design?

Have you ever wondered what it takes to design and build a roller coaster? At last, there's a book that shows you. A mix of engineering and art, roller coasters are complex three-dimensional puzzles consisting of thousands of individual parts. Designers spend countless hours creating and tweaking ride paths to push the envelope of exhilaration, all while maintaining the highest safety standards. ***Coasters 101: An Engineering Guide to Roller Coaster Design*** examines the numerous diverse aspects of roller coaster engineering, including some of the mathematical formulas and engineering concepts used.

A few of the topics covered include:

- ❖ Design Software and Computer Technology
- ❖ Project Management
- ❖ Wheel Design and Material Selection
- ❖ Track Fabrication Techniques
- ❖ Daily Inspections and Preventive Maintenance
- ❖ Amusement Industry Safety Standards
- ❖ Career Advice

And much more!

This technical guide is the most detailed roller coaster design book to date and will take you through the entire process, from concept to creation. A must read for every enthusiast and aspiring roller coaster engineer!

Get **Coasters 101: An Engineering Guide to Roller Coaster Design** from Amazon.com today.

Did You Like The 50 Most Unique Roller Coasters Ever Built?

Before you go, I'd like to say "thank you" for purchasing my book. I know you could have picked from dozens of other books but you took a chance on mine. So a big thanks for ordering this book and reading all the way to the end.

Now I'd like to ask for a *small* favor. Could you please take a minute or two and leave a review for this book on Amazon.com? Your comments are really valuable because they will guide future editions of this book and I'm always striving to improve my writing.

About the Author

Nick Weisenberger is currently co-manager of Coaster101.com as well as a member of the ASTM International F-24 committee on Amusement Rides and Devices. He's ridden over one hundred and fifty different coasters and in August 2009, he participated in the Coasting for Kids Ride-a-thon where he endured a ten hour marathon ride (that's 105 laps) and helped raise over $10,000 for Give Kids the World charity. When not writing or working, Nick likes to read, hike, watch football, and explore. An avid traveler, look for Nick on the midways of your local amusement park!

What to know more? Drop by and check out Coaster101.com, a growing resource and community for roller coaster enthusiasts, aspiring students, and theme park fans.

Questions or comments? Email me: **nick@coaster101.com**

Or feel free to say hi on Twitter (@NTWProductions).

Appendix I: Glossary

4th Dimension: Controlled rotatable seats cantilevered on each side of the track.

Airtime: Roller coasters can thrust negative Gs on riders causing them to momentarily lift off their seats and become "weightless." As the vehicle flies over the top of a hill the load on the passenger becomes less than Earth's gravity and, in the extreme, could throw an unrestrained passenger out of the car. Scream machines with oodles of so-called "airtime" moments or "butterflies in your stomach" thrills rank among the world's best. Negative g-forces cannot be too great because when under high negative g forces blood rushed to the head and can cause "red out."

Block: A block is a section of a roller coaster's track with a controllable start and stop point. Only one train may occupy a block at a time.

Bobsled: Cars travel freely down a U-shaped track (no rails) like a bobsled except on wheels.

Bunny Hops: A series of small hills engineered to give repeated doses of airtime

Cobra roll: A half-loop followed by half a corkscrew, then another half corkscrew into another half-loop. The trains are inverted twice and exit the element the opposite direction in which they entered.

Corkscrew: A loop where the entrance and exit points have been stretched apart.

Cycle: When the train completes one circuit around the course. When trains are run continuously this is called cycling.

Dark ride: An indoor ride, usually slow moving through sets based on a central theme, sometime will feature interactivity like shooting at targets

Dive loop: The track twists upward and to the side, similar to half a corkscrew, before diving towards the ground in a half-loop. Basically, the opposite of an Immelman inversion.

Dueling: Two separate tracks but mostly not parallel. Usually contain several head-on, near miss collision sensations.

Floorless: The vehicle sits above the track but contains no floor between the rider's feet and the rails, allowing their legs to dangle freely.

G force: G force is expressed as a ratio of the force developed in changing speed or direction relative to the force felt due to the Earth's gravity. The smaller the curve radius and the higher the speed, the greater the g-force felt. Thus, a 2g force on a 100 pound body causes it to weigh 200 pounds (Weight = Mass x G Force). Indianapolis 500 racers are subjected to more than 3g's in the corners of their hairpin turns while there are looping coasters that subject passengers to as much as 6g's. Positive g-forces, meaning those that push your butt into the seat, become uncomfortable for the human body at +5g and may cause the loss of consciousness.

Giga coaster: Any roller coaster with at least one element between 300 and 399 feet tall.

Hyper coaster: Any roller coaster with at least one element between 200 and 299 feet tall.

Imagineer: A person who works for Walt Disney Imagineering. This word is a combination of engineer and imagination.

Immelman: Named after the aircraft maneuver pioneered by Max Immelman, the inversion begins with a vertical loop but at the apex of the inversion turns into a corkscrew exiting at the side instead of completing the loop. The opposite of a dive loop element.

Inversion: An element on a roller coaster track which turns riders 180 degrees upside down and then rights them again, such as a loop, corkscrew, or barrel roll (among others).

Inverted: Vehicle is fixed below the rails with rider's feet hanging freely and is able to invert upside down.

Laydown/Flying: Riders are parallel to the rails, either on their back or stomach.

Mobius: A racing or dueling roller coaster with one

continuous track instead of two separate ones.

Motorbike: Riders straddle the seats as if riding a motorcycle, jet ski, or horse.

Pipeline: Riders are positioned between the rails instead of above or below them.

Queue: A line you stand in for an attraction, food, or entry/exit.

Racing Coaster: Two separate tracks usually parallel for most of the course. Trains are released simultaneously so they race from start to finish.

Sit down: Traditional roller coaster with vehicles above the rails.

Spinning: Seats can freely spin on a horizontal axis.

Standup: Riders are restrained in a standing position.

Swinging suspended: The vehicle hangs below the rails and can freely swing from side to side but does not invert.

Themed: The central idea or concept for an attraction or area.

THRC: Theoretical Hourly Ride Capacity is the number of guests per hour that can experience an attraction under optimal operating conditions. Calculated by: Riders per bench*benches per car*cars per train*(60min/ride time minutes).

Wingrider: The seats are fixed on both sides of the vehicle outside of the rails.

Appendix II: Acronyms

The following is a list of acronyms found within this text and includes common terms used throughout the amusement industry (in alphabetical order).

ACE: American Coaster Enthusiasts
ARB: Anti-Roll Back
ASTM: American Society of Standards and Materials
CAD: Computer Aided Design
CPM: Critical Path Method
FEA: Finite Element Analysis
FMEA: Failure Mode and Effects Analysis
FTA: Fault Tree Analysis
GDT: Geometrical Dimension and Tolerance
IAAPA: International Association of Amusement Parks and Attractions
ISO: International Organization for Standardization
LIM: Linear Induction Motor
LOTO: Lock Out Tag Out
LSM: Linear Synchronous Motor
MBD: Model Based Definition
MTBF: Mean Time Between Failures
MTTR: Mean Time To Repair
OEM: Original Equipment Manufacturer
OSHA: Occupational Safety and Health Administration
OSS: Operator Safety System
PERT: Project Evaluation and Review Technique
PLC: Programmable Logic Controller
POV: Point of View
RA: Ride Analysis
RAC: Ride Access Control
RCDB: Roller Coaster Data Base
SBNO: Standing But Not Operating
SLC: Suspended Looping Coaster
SRCS: Safety Related Control Systems
T&A: Test and Adjust
THRC: Theoretical Hourly Ride Capacity

Appendix III: Resources

American Coaster Enthusiasts (ACE)
http://www.aceonline.org/

ASTM International
http://www.ASTM.org

Amusement Industry Manufacturers and Suppliers (AIMS)
http://www.aimsintl.org/

International Association of Amusement Parks and Aquariums (IAAPA)
http://www.IAAPA.org/

Coaster101
http://www.Coaster101.com

Roller Coaster Database
http://www.RCDB.com

Photography Credits

Pictures by Nick Weisenberger:
Lost Coaster at Indiana Beach
FireChaser Express at Dollywood
Jet Star 2 at Lagoon Park
Flying Turns at Knoebels

Pictures by John Stevenson:
Hades 360 at Mount Olympus
Goliath at Six Flags Great America

Pictures by Patrick McGarvey
Maverick at Cedar Point

Flickr Pictures distributed under a Cc-BY 2.0 License:
http://creativecommons.org/licenses/by/2.0/

Z-Force Roller Coaster by Joel, https://flic.kr/p/nDFhBs
BonBon-Land's Dog Fart Coaster by Martin Lewison, **https://flic.kr/p/8357sh**
Cobra caught in the loop by Kecko, https://flic.kr/p/7NLR34
Cobra Start-up by Kecko, https://flic.kr/p/7NLVe6
Verbolten - Busch Gardens, Williamsburg by brownpau, https://flic.kr/p/fNJb6U
Battlestar Galactica by Jo N, **https://flic.kr/p/7QaPYw**
Scooby Doo Spooky Coaster, Movie World, Gold Coast by Widhi Rachmanto, https://flic.kr/p/b1mSpn
Furius Baco by Jordi Payà, https://flic.kr/p/chTAZ5
Yas Waterworld - Abu Dhabi by Sarah Ackerman, https://flic.kr/p/eafmAp, https://flic.kr/p/eam4mf
Six Flags Magic Mountain 104 by Jeremy Thompson, https://flic.kr/p/9awXyB
Hard Rock Park 067 by Jeremy Thompson, https://flic.kr/p/5MHr8c
Rollercoaster by Joanna Chlasta, https://flic.kr/p/d3658J

Exiting the station on Big Grizzly Mountain by Megan, https://flic.kr/p/dXxrN1

Tornado by Sarah Ackerman, **https://flic.kr/p/8oFigE**

Euro Mir by Oliver Mallich, https://flic.kr/p/pcgCW

Lightwater Valley 039 by Jeremy Thompson, https://flic.kr/p/8bqWAn

Lightwater valley 031 by Jeremy Thompson, **https://flic.kr/p/8bqScK**

G-Force (Drayton Manor) by Michael Welsing, https://flic.kr/p/4mLJPx

Blackpool Pleasure Beach 106 by Jeremy Thompson, https://flic.kr/p/8feg4L

Atlantis Adventure Aqua Trax! by Martin Lewison, https://flic.kr/p/5oyXHa

The crane by Margo Akermark, https://flic.kr/p/6HwmhP

Printed in Great Britain
by Amazon

85089452R00063